THE SAINT AND RETURN OF THE SAINT COLLECTABLES

John Buss

AMBERLEY

Acknowledgements

I would like to thank the following for their assistance in the preparation of this book: Louise Harker at Vectis Toy Auctions; Remco Admiraal for assistance in tracking down many of the European items that otherwise would have escaped me; Jaz Wiseman for his assistance on *Return of the Saint* memorabilia; and Stuart James McKell.

First published 2022

Amberley Publishing
The Hill, Stroud
Gloucestershire, GL5 4EP

www.amberley-books.com

Copyright © John Buss, 2022

The right of John Buss to be identified as the Author of this work has been asserted in accordance with the Copyrights, Designs and Patents Act 1988.

ISBN 978 1 3981 0125 8 (print)
ISBN 978 1 3981 0126 5 (ebook)

British Library Cataloguing in Publication Data.
A catalogue record for this book is available from the British Library.

Typeset in 10pt on 13pt Celeste.
Typesetting by SJmagic DESIGN SERVICES, India.
Printed in the UK.

Contents

Introduction

Simon Templar, otherwise known as the Saint, first created by Leslie Charteris in his 1928 novel, *Meet the Tiger,* was also the star of both a series of feature films and radio series in the late 1930s and early 1940s. The major collectables for the Saint must, of course, be the novels and magazines that feature the Saint. This book, though, is primarily looking at the wealth of merchandise to accompany the television incarnations of the notorious Simon Templar, primarily Roger Moore who played him from 1962–1969, and Ian Ogilvy who took on the role during the 1970s.

The Saint, a kind of modern-day Robin Hood, or Raffles, a gentleman, debonair charmer, not entirely honest, but always morally on the side of good. Taking the name of 'the Saint' from his initials ST, the Saint globe-trotted around the world. He could turn up anywhere, at any time, almost always at odds with the local law enforcement agencies.

The Saint tackled adversaries, so detached from their crimes that no legal method could ever touch them. He went to the heart of the problem; the crooked financiers, drug dealers, gun runners, etc., those who reaped the financial rewards of crime, whilst never dirtying their hands. He, of course, made sure he was well paid for his services in dealing out justice. The Saint was the first in a new breed of modern hero, those who work outside the law almost considering themselves above it.

Above left: USA poster *The Fiction Makers.*

Above right: Turkish poster *Vendetta for the Saint.*

Above: Italian poster *The Fiction Makers*.

Right: USA paperback *The Saint in the Sun*.

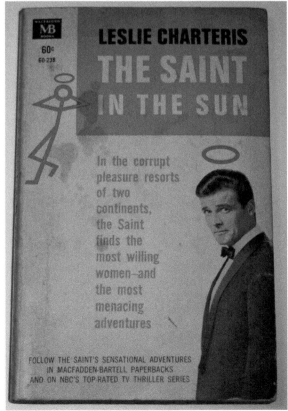

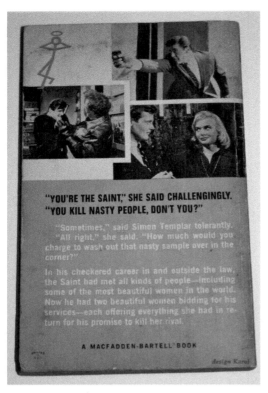

USA paperback reverse.

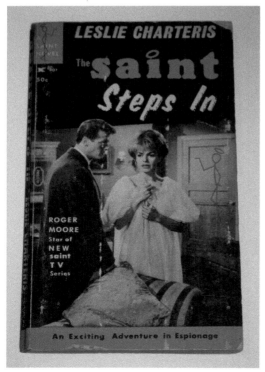

USA paperback *The Saint Steps In.*

The Saint ITC 1962–1969

Enter the TV Saint

Long having resisted television's advances with regards to a TV version of the Saint, Leslie Charteris was eventually persuaded by Lew Grade, enabling his company, ITC, to launch production on what was to become one of ITV's biggest hit shows of the 1960s.

The first series aired in the UK in 1962 and was an almost instant success. Roger Moore was perfectly cast as the suave, sophisticated Simon Templar. Initially the episodes were adaptations of the popular Saint novels, though in a slightly tamed down incarnation for the small screen. Moore's Saint is a more likeable rogue than the far more egotistical and aloof Saint of the Charteris novels. As was inevitable, the producers soon ran out of novels to adapt, so later episodes consisted of entirely new stories.

In total Roger Moore starred in 118 episodes of *The Saint*, which were produced between 1962 and 1969. The first seventy-one were filmed in black and white, then with the sale of episodes to the American NBC network, a further forty-seven colour episodes were made. Bamoore produced these later colour episodes for ITC, a company co-owned by the series star Roger Moore.

Interestingly the bulk of memorabilia for this series seems to be of the paper variety with very little in the way of toys.

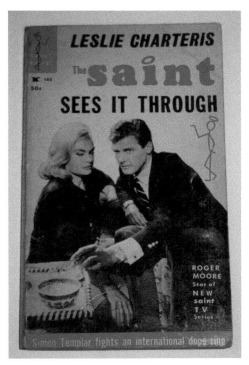

USA paperback *The Saint Sees it Through.*

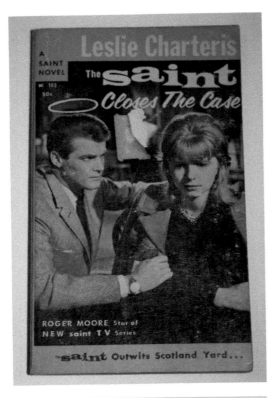

USA paperback *The Saint Closes the Case.*

USA paperback *The Avenging Saint.*

Books and Annuals

American Paperbacks

It was inevitable given the success of *The Saint* TV series that many of the original Charteris Saint novels would gain a new lease of life. In the USA at least fifteen novels were reissued in paperback form with Roger Moore photo covers. These American reprints were almost all published by the Fiction Publishing Company of New York, though the first American paperback to tie in with the series was issued by Macfadden Bartell in 1966. This was *The Saint in the Sun.* As well as Roger Moore featuring on the front cover, the back cover also features a nice array of photographs from the series. Quite why they only produced one tie in paperback before the Fiction Publishing Company took over releasing television related Saint titles is unknown. All of the issues from this company appear to date from 1967. The first in this series was *The Saint Steps In.* This was followed by *The Saint Sees it Through, The Saint Closes the Case, The Avenging Saint, Saint's Getaway, The Saint in New York,*

Above left: USA paperback *Saint's Getaway.*

Above right: USA paperback *The Saint in New York.*

Above left: USA paperback *Enter the Saint*.

Above right: USA paperback *The Saint Meets his Match*.

Left: USA paperback *Featuring the Saint*.

Above left: USA paperback *Alias the Saint*.

Above right: USA paperback *The Saint Overboard*.

Right: USA paperback *The Brighter Buccaneer*.

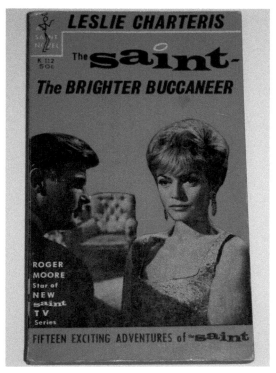

USA paperback *The Saint vs Scotland Yard.*

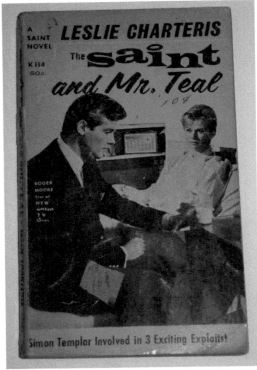

USA paperback *The Saint and Mr Teal.*

12

Enter the Saint, The Saint Meets his Match, Featuring the Saint, Alias the Saint, The Saint Overboard, The Saint the Brighter Buccaneer, The Saint vs Scotland Yard and *The Saint and Mr Teal.* All of these paperbacks had an original cover price of 50 cents.

Spanish Paperbacks

The Saint was immensely popular around the world and in Spain the Spanish publisher Cabello Negro issued ten paperbacks to tie into the series. Unlike the American books, which each featured a different photographic cover, these Spanish issues were quite dull in comparison. Each cover features exactly the same black and white photograph. *El Santo* features in a different colour on each title with just the position of the stickman varying from cover to cover. The Spanish titles issued were *El Santo en era una Dama, El Santo contra el Tigre, El Santo contra la Policia, Entra el Santo, El Santo en la Evasion, El Santo en la Jugada (Para Pillo, Pillo Y Medio), El Santo en el Ultimo Heroe, El Santo en la hija del Millonario, Otra vez el Santo, Alias el Santo.*

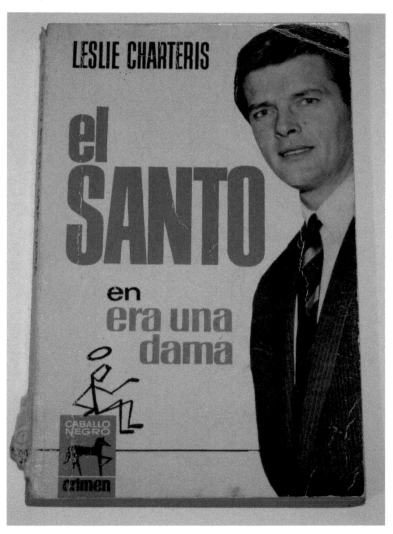

Spanish paperback
*El Santo en era
una dama.*

13

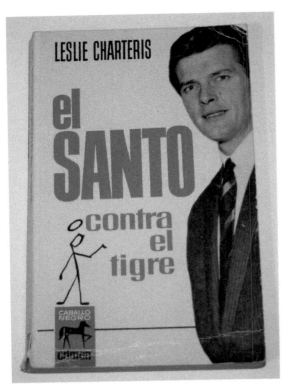

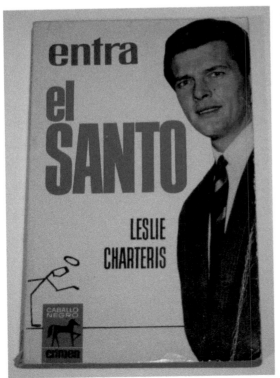

Above left: Spanish paperback *El Santo contra el Tigre.*

Above right: Spanish paperback *El Santo contra la Policia.*

Left: Spanish paperback *Entra el Santo.*

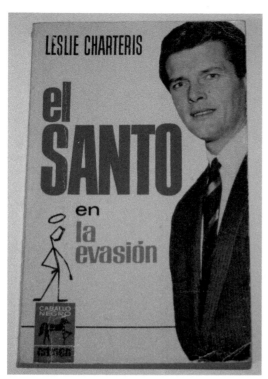

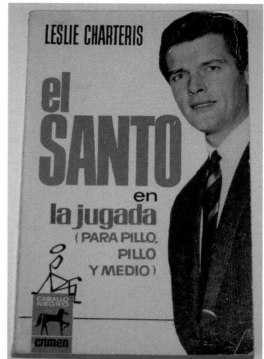

Above left: Spanish paperback *El Santo en la Evasion.*

Above right: Spanish paperback *El Santo n la Jugada* (*Para Pillo, Pillo Y Medio*).

Right: Spanish paperback *El Santo en el ultimo Heroe.*

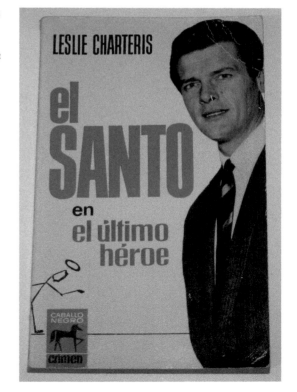

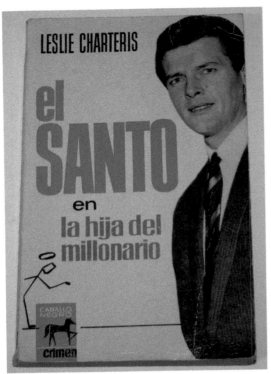

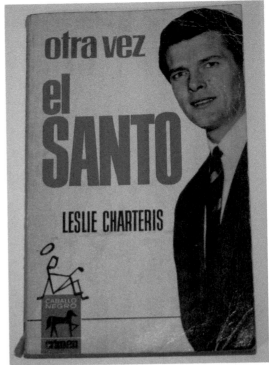

Above left: Spanish paperback *El Santo la hija dl millonario.*

Above right: Spanish paperback *Otra vez el Santo.*

Left: Spanish paperback *Alias el Santo.*

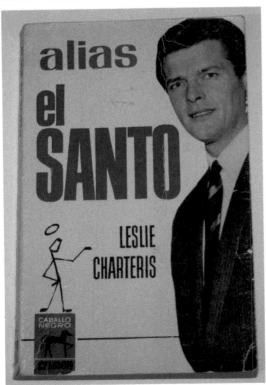

Portuguese Paperbacks

Portugal also saw at least three of the Saint novels reissued to tie into the Roger Moore TV series. These were published by Livros do Brasil in their Colecceo Vampiro series. The titles were *O Santo e o Milionário Invisível, O Santo em Miami* and *O Santo em Lonres*.

Portuguese paperback *O Santo em Miami*. (Remco Admiraal)

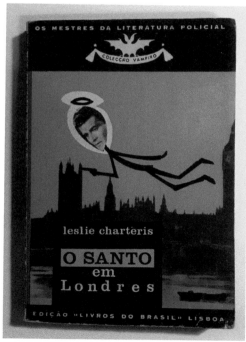

Portuguesa paperback *O Santo em Lonres*. (Remco Admiraal)

Danish Paperbacks

In Denmark there were six paperbacks published by Carit Andersens Forlag. All six novels have an identical back cover photograph of Roger Moore as the Saint. Titles in the Danish series were *Helgenen og den vilde jagt* (*The Saint's Getaway*), *Helgenen tager Affære* (*The Saint Steps In*), *Stol på Helgenen* (*Trust the Saint*), *Helgenen Griber Ind* (this book features stories from several Saint titles including *The King of the Beggars* and *The Bunco Artists*), *Helgenen slår Til* (contains the stories *The Black Market* and *The Careful Terrorist*), *Helgenen tager Hævn* (*Vendetta for the Saint*).

Danish paperback *Halgenen tager affaere.* (Remco Admiraal)

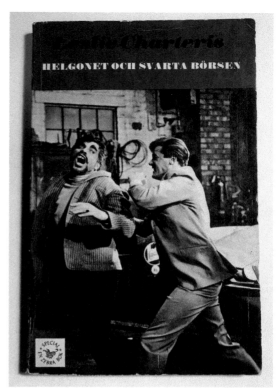

Above left: Danish paperback *Helenen griber ind* (Remco Admiraal)

Above right: Swedish paperback. (Remco Admiraal)

Swedish Paperback
There is also at least one Swedish paperback *Helgonet Och Svarta Borsen*. Published as an En Zebra Bok special that features a Roger Moore cover.

British Annuals
No such TV related reissues of the novels appear to have been released in the UK, though other directly television related books did appear, including three annuals by World Distributors Ltd. The first of these annuals was produced in 1967, with the others following in 1968 and 1969. None of these annuals have a date displayed upon the cover, but they are copy written inside.

The Saint Annual (© 1967) World Distributors
This first annual features a red cover with an illustration of Moore wearing a blue jumper. There is a white flash across the lower half of the cover, with a line drawing of the Volvo P1800 being pursued by another vehicle. This annual contains a strong line-up of original text stories, such as 'The Saint and the Face Gang', 'The Room That Wasn't' and 'The Jackdaw Plays Diamonds', while the features and games included have a very tenuous connection, if any, to the show. This first annual was priced at 10/6d.

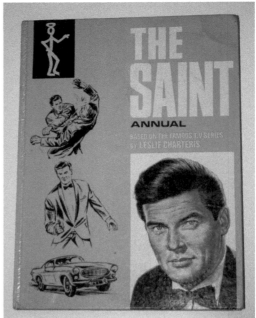

1967 British annual.   1968 British annual.

The Saint Annual (©1968) World Distributors
This second annual features a blue cover with line drawings of the Saint in action along the left-hand side. In the bottom right corner is an illustration of Moore as the Saint, above this is the title in white. This annual contains a very similar mixture of original text stories and features to World Distributors' previous annual, while the price has had to increase to 12/6*d*.

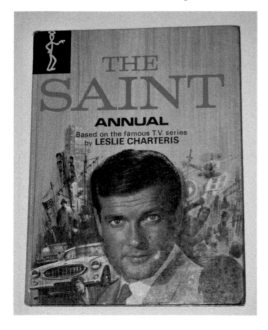

1969 British annual.

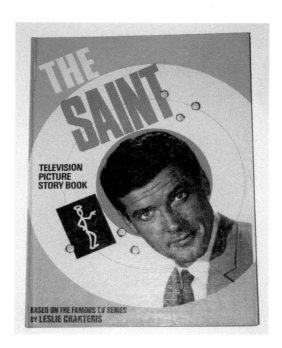

The Saint Television Picture Story Book.

The Saint Annual (© 1969) World Distributors

This was the last of the annuals based on the series to be released and features a woodgrain effect upon the cover, with a photograph of Roger Moore overlaid upon illustrated action scenes. For the first time this annual featured both strip stories as well as text stories, along with an assortment of features. The price of 12/6d was retained.

The Saint Television Picture Storybook PBS Ltd (©1971)

One other annual-sized book was produced in the UK, this was *The Saint Television Picture Story Book*, published by PBS Ltd in 1971. This book features a blue cover with a photograph of Roger Moore in the centre surrounded by a white target. It contains a mixture of text and strip stories, all of which appear to have been reprinted from the 1969 World Distributors' annual.

New Novels

The television series, having run out of original Charteris novels, had commissioned various writers to invent new adventures for the series. Several of these were later adapted by Fleming Lee, with Leslie Charteris editing, into new Saint novels. In the UK these hardbacks were published by Hodder and Stoughton Ltd, while paperbacks were by Hodder paperbacks.

The first of these new novels was *The Saint on TV*, published in 1968. It featured adaptations of two television episodes, 'The Death Game' and 'The Power Artist'.

Also published in 1968, the second new Saint novel, was *The Fiction Makers*, which was based on a two-part story from the series. This pair of episodes also saw release in several countries including the USA as a feature film.

Another new novel released in the UK based on television episodes was *The Saint Abroad*, published in 1969. This novel contained adaptations of the television episodes 'The Art Collectors' and 'The Persistent Patriots'.

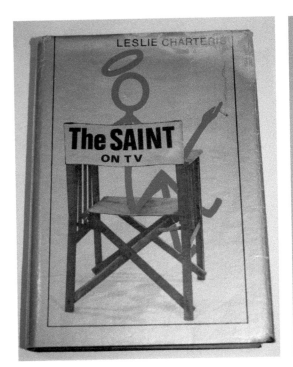

Above left: *The Saint on TV* hardback.

Above right: *The Saint on TV* paperback.

Left: *The Saint and the People Importers* hardback.

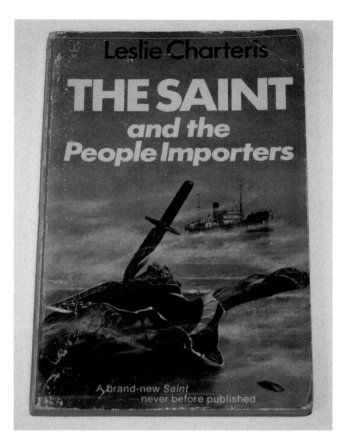

The Saint and the People Importers paperback.

The USA also saw the release of several new novels, which were published by Doubleday. Once again these are all adaptations of TV episodes, and again are written by Fleming Lee, being edited by Leslie Charteris. The 1968 UK Hodder and Stoughton Ltd books release *The Fiction Makers*, now titled *The Saint and the Fiction Makers*, was published in the USA. The other USA releases were *The Saint Returns*, also released in 1968, and *The Saint and the People Importers* released in 1971.

The People Importers did also see publication in the UK in 1971 as well, both in hardback – Hodder and Stoughton Ltd again – and a paperback edition, published by Hodder paperbacks. This story wasn't so much an adaptation of the TV episode as it was the author's own exploration of their idea. Charteris had outlined an idea to Fleming Lee, who then wrote the synopsis that was given to the TV production, but rather than employing him to write the script, as Charteris had suggested, other writers were employed and changed things considerably. When it came to the novel Charteris and Lee reverted back to their original synopsis to quote the foreword 'ignoring the Television 'improvements'.

Other Books and Annuals

Due to its popularity, and that of its star Roger Moore, *The Saint* featured not only in these directly related titles but in a whole host of other books and annuals. Many of these other annual sized titles do not display a year on the cover so copyright dates where known are given.

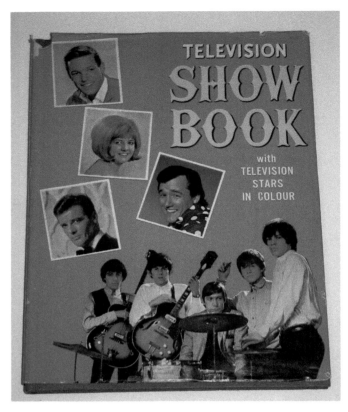

Television Show Book 1965.

Purnell books included features and photographs of the series in both their *ATV Television Show Book* and *ATV Television Star Book* (both © 1963). The same company once again included articles and photographs of Roger Moore and the Saint in the following years *Television Show Book* (© 1964) which has a dust jacket featuring the Beatles. Published at a price of 10/6d. Likewise, the same years *Television Star Book* (Dave Clark 5 on Cover) published at 5/- included similar.

In 1965 the series featured in the *Boyfriend Book* from *City Magazines* published at a cost of 10/6d. This book very much aimed at the teen girl market of the time. Purnell's 1965 *Television Show Book* featured an image of Roger Moore as the Saint with an inside feature on the series.

While the *Television Stars* book (© 1966) from Purnell, would again contain photographs and features about *The Saint*. This book has a colour dust jacket featuring photographs of *Danger Man, The Man from U.N.C.L.E.* and others.

Next up is the *Roger Moore Adventure Book* (© 1966) published by Panther Books/ Souvenir Press. This only has passing connection to *The Saint*, being published at the height of Roger Moore's popularity as this character on TV at the time. It does, however, have one directly related article entitled 'Self Defence and the Saint'. Books like this also open up the tricky question of where to draw the line between collecting items from the series and those related to the shows lead actor. Can, for example, knitting patterns that Roger Moore modelled for be considered as collectables for the series. The original price for the *Roger Moore Adventure Book* was 12/6d.

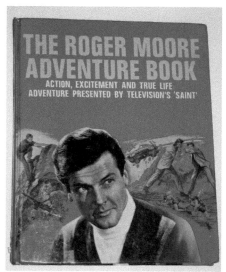

Above left: *The Roger Moore Adventure Book*.

Above right: Knitting patterns.

   Star TV & Film Annual 1967 featured Roger Moore on its cover and contained a feature on *The Saint*. Likewise, Roger Moore also appeared on the cover, but not inside the undated *Television Stars* book from Purnell publishing.
   The Saint was a regular comic strip in the *TV Tornado* comic for most of its run (more details later) and featured in four annuals based on the comic. All four annuals were published by World Distributors Ltd. Each annual contains a mixture of features, text and strip stories based on the popular television series of the period. The first one came out in 1967.

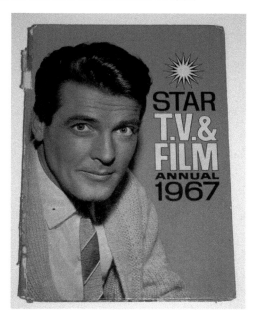

Star TV & Film Annual 1967.

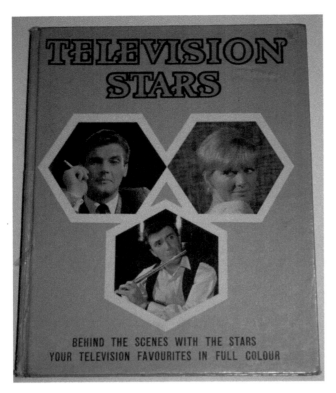

Undated *Television Stars* book.

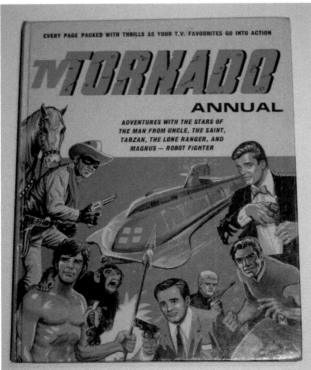

TV Tornado Annual 1969.

TV Tornado Annual (© 1967) World Distributors
This annual originally priced at 10/6*d* features *The Saint* upon its cover and contained a text Saint story entitled 'The Silver Chute'.

TV Tornado Annual (© 1968) World Distributors
The Saint is once again on the cover of the 1968 annual which also featured two Saint stories, a text story 'Bag of Tricks' and a comic strip story 'Sinister Castle'.

TV Tornado Annual (1969) World Distributors
The third *TV Tornado Annual*, from 1969, with the Saint making it on the cover montage once again, also featured images of *The Man from U.N.C.L.E.*, *Tarzan*, *The Lone Ranger* and *Voyage to the Bottom of the Sea*. The cover price for this annual and the following years increased to 12/6*d*. While the Saint story contained was 'Blast-off Midnight', which appeared in comic strip form.

TV Tornado Annual (© 1970) World Distributors Ltd
The fourth and final *TV Tornado Annual*. Once again, the Saint appeared as part of the montage cover, which also featured *Tarzan*, *The High Chaparral*, *The Lone Ranger* and

TV Tornado Annual 1970.

Voyage to the Bottom of the Sea along with several others, whilst the back cover had a line drawing of Tarzan. The artwork within this annual is an acquired taste. Two Saint stories, one text 'Double First for the Saint' and one strip story 'All you Rings you Keeps'.

TV 21 Annual 1971

When *TV Tornado* merged into the *TV 21* comic, *The Saint* was one of the few items that continued, so it was natural that it would appear in the 1971 *TV 21* Annual, which it did in the form of a strip story 'The Saint Meets the Mad-masters'. Roger Moore would also appear on the front cover of the very first *Look-in* annual in the same year.

Moving into the early 1970s *The Saint* appears less as in its own right and more as a passing reference in features about Roger Moore, with the emphasis turning more towards Roger's newest TV show *The Persuaders*. This is the case with the 1972 *All Star Television Annual* from Panda Publishing, which includes an article on Roger Moore.

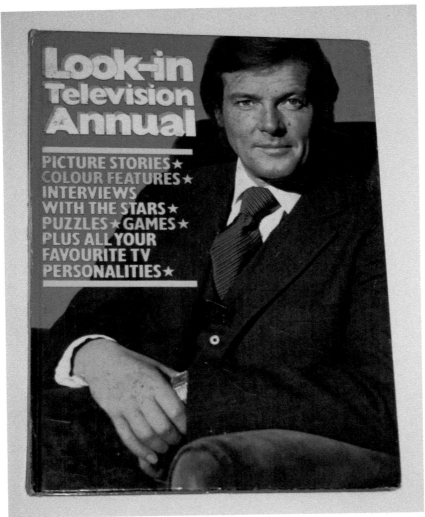

Look-in Annual 1971.

Toys and Games

Corgi Toys

The Saint's Volvo P1800 Corgi Toys 1965

One of the things most associated with the Saint of the 1960s were his wheels, in particular the white Volvo P1800, Reg. No ST1, a nice, discreet, inconspicuous little car. The car used for the series was especially flown in by Volvo as no white models of the P1800 were in the country, and by all accounts Roger Moore was so taken by it he purchased one for own use.

Above: Corgi Saint Volvo No. 258.

Right: Corgi Saint Volvo No. 258 with no interior.

This car has the distinction of being the first television related model to be produced by Corgi Toys. Marcel R. Van Cleemput, the former chief designer at Corgi Toys, spoke about its introduction into the Corgi range:

Well as you know it all started with the very first model *The Saint*, The Saint Volvo. I can't really remember why we decided to do that, we'd got a Volvo in the range and of course the programme was quite popular and it was sort of a quick way to get into

Corgi Saint Volvo No. 258 with ridged wheels. (Vectis)

Corgi Saint Volvo No. 258 Blue Bonnet. (Vectis)

30

the market put a label of The Saint on the bonnet and there we were, it proved very successful. That obviously wets the appetite and you want to do more. So we followed on with other things. At Corgis we were always inventive we were the first with virtually every type of feature on the market. Then we saw *The Saint* on television and we had a Volvo already in the range we thought it would be a good way to capitalise on the programme, which we did with just adding a label and it was very successful. So after that we had to look around and carry on adding more character merchandise.

Several different versions of this model appeared over the years. The first issued in March 1965 was just a plain white model with the stick logo on the bonnet. It proved so successful

Corgi Saint Volvo No. 258 red bonnet spun wheels. (Vectis)

Corgi Saint Volvo No. 201 white bonnet whizzwheels. (Vectis)

(over 300,000 sold in the first year) it was to open the floodgates of TV related tie ins from the firm (the James Bond Aston Martin following very closely on its heels, then U.N.C.L.E., Batman, etc.). Some of these Volvos have been found with no interior whatsoever, but it normally came with a moulded interior and a figure of the Saint driving. There are also variants that have ridged wheels, as opposed to a plain spun wheel. This original issue Corgi reference 258 came in a solid card box at an original price 3/11d. In more recent years, versions of this model have started to appear with a blue bonnet the same as the Corgi Rockets model.

The Saints Volvo P1800 Corgi Toys 1970

The Volvo was reissued in 1970 with a new reference number 201. This second issue differed from the previous release. Having whizzwheels as opposed to the spun metal wheels with tyres on first issue, and a red sticker on the bonnet with *The Saint* logo in the

Corgi Saint Volvo No. 201 red bonnet tyred wheels red spindle. (Vectis)

Corgi Saint Volvo No. 201 red bonnet whizz wheels. (Vectis)

centre. Otherwise, the car is as per previous issue. Versions of this model have also been seen with different wheels, these being tyred with a red central spindle. The original price on this issue was 5/11d. This model, unlike its predecessor, came in a window-style box.

Corgi Toys Gift Set 48

This car transporter gift set contains the earlier, tyred version of the Saint Volvo, but with a later red bonnet. This short-lived gift set was actually the first usage of the new red bonneted version of the Saint Volvo. The set was issued in May of 1969 and was, according to Marcel R. Van Cleemput, withdrawn within a few months (later in 1969). Interestingly, as late as 1973 both this set, and Gift Set 20 appear side by side in the Corgi catalogue. The set contained Corgi's newly produced car transporter and along with the Saint's Volvo

Corgi GS 48 first issue box. (Vectis)

Corgi GS 48 second issue box. (Vectis)

33

Corgi catalogue 1973.

the other cars issued within the set were: an MGC GT, Monte Carlo Mini-Cooper, Monte Carlo Imp, Mini-Cooper 'Magnifique' and a Morris Mini-Minor. There appear to be two different issues of this set, the first is in a solid box with an artwork lid and contains the Saints Volvo, while the second edition has a window box similar to Gift Set 20 but does not contain the Volvo.

Corgi Toys Gift Set 41

Another car transporter and cars set produced by Corgi Toys. This set contained a Carrimore Mk IV transporter with MGC GT, Hillman Imp, Wickerwork Mini, Monte Carlo Mini, Morris Mini Minor and the red bonneted version of the Saint's Volvo with spun wheels. It features nearly identical box artwork to Gift Set 48 and was probably released in late 1969 or early 1970, and goes completely unmentioned in this configuration in Marcel R. Van Cleemput's writings on Corgi Toys.

Corgi GS 41. (Vectis)

Corgi GS 20. (Vectis)

Corgi Toys Gift Set 20

Following the withdrawal of Gift Set 48, Corgi introduced a new Car Transporter gift set in October of 1970. This later set contained vehicles with the new whizzwheels, including the newly reissued Saint Volvo with whizzwheels and red bonnet. Along with the Saint Volvo, the set contained a Scammell handyman Mk III tractor unit with a Carrimore Tri-deck Mk V transporter. This model was one of Corgi's major new releases that year. The other cars in the set consisted of a Lancia Fulvia sport Zagato, Marcos 3-litre, MGC GT, Ford Capri V6 3-litre and a Pontiac Firebird. This set had a longer lifespan than its predecessor, being withdrawn in 1973.

Corgi Rockets

Corgi produced one other model of the Saint Volvo, which was in their Corgi Rockets range. Corgi Rockets were Corgi's short-lived attempt at combating the threat of Mattel's Hot Wheels, which by the late 1960s were just arriving into the UK. Corgi Rockets had what Corgi called 'extra play value'. The chassis and even the whole axel assembly were removable and inter-changeable between model cars within the range; a range which also included several James Bond models. These models were built to a smaller size, being about the same size as the Corgi Jr range. The white Saint Volvo model in this series featured a blue bonnet with the familiar stick man logo in the centre. Minor variations in the packaging for this exist. Some models have the car bubble packed side on to the card, while others have the car wheels down on the card allowing for better display of the model.

The Corgi Rockets version of the car would also appear in an 'autobatic speedset', which as well as the car contained a 16-ft-long section of track with loop-the-loop and jump for

35

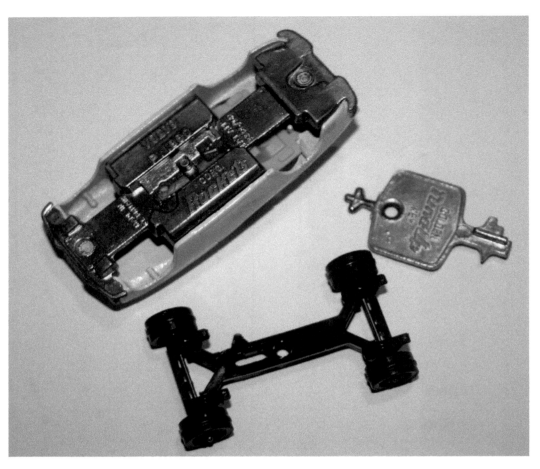

Above: Corgi Rockets chassis dismantled.

Left: Corgi Rockets bubble pack style 1.

Right: Corgi
Rockets bubble
pack style 2.
(Vectis)

Below: Autobatic
Speedset box.

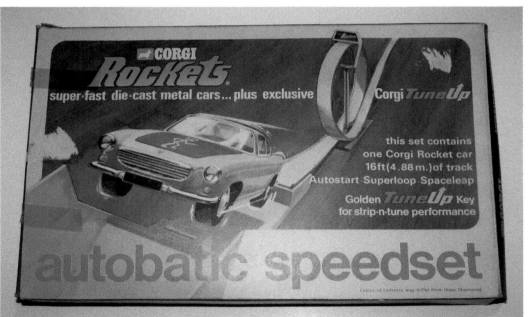

Autobatic Speedset box detail.

the car to negotiate. This was not actually sold as a Saint toy, but it contained the Saint's Volvo P1800 and the car is also illustrated on the box. Issued in 1969, the set was originally priced at 30/2*d*.

Jigsaws by Tower Press 1966

A range of four jigsaws was produced in 1966 by the firm Tower Press. These puzzles are packaged in a yellow box showing a black and white photograph of Roger Moore, and the design contained within, on the box front. The rear of the box as is normal for many jigsaws of the period and shows the four different designs available in the set. Each puzzle in the series contained approx. 240 pieces and was sized around 14.5 inches by 9.5. Puzzles were priced at 1/11 1/2*d*.

The four puzzles in the set were: 1) Ambushed by Smugglers, 2) Adventure in Dockland, 3) Chopper to the Rescue and 4) Attacked from All Sides.

38

Jigsaw 1.

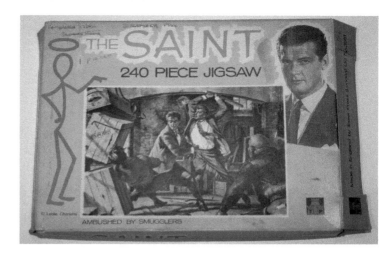

Jigsaw 2.

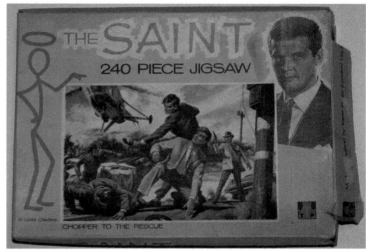

Jigsaw 3.

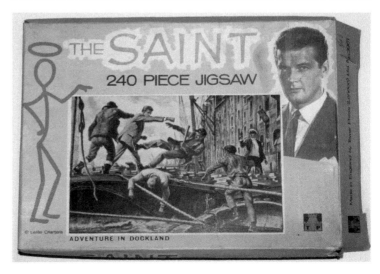

Jigsaw 4.

Lone Star Items

The firm Lone Star appear to have produced several items relating to the Roger Moore series starting with the obligatory toy gun.

The Saint's Pistol Lone Star 1966

Child's cap gun made of die-cast metal, shaped like a Luger 9 mm automatic. It came complete with removable silencer and large impressive telescopic sight. This was exactly the same as the later issue U.N.C.L.E. gun from the same firm. In both cases the only thing to show the item is connected with a TV series is a small label stuck to the side of the gun naming the series. This came presented on a brightly coloured backing card. The silencer in all of the 1966 Lone Star Saint sets is of a long thin type.

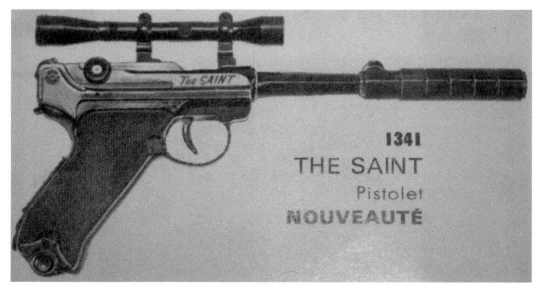

First style Lone Star Pistol in French catalogue.

40

1342 "THE SAINT" GUN & HOLSTER SET

A leather shoulder holster made specially for "The Saint" Pistol with a single adjustable strap. The Holster is fitted with a carrying case for the Silencer and retaining strap for the Telescopic Sight. Individually carded.

First style Lone Star Pistol & Holster set in catalogue.

The Saint's Gun and Holster Set Lone Star, 1966

The same pistol was also issued with a faux leather shoulder holster made especially for the Saint pistol with a white single adjustable strap. The holster is fitted with a carrying case for the silencer, and a retainer strap for the telescopic sight. It also features the Saint stick man in white on its side.

The Saint Laboratory Set Lone Star, 1966

This appears to have been a large cased set similar to those issued for U.N.C.L.E. Some doubt as to if it was ever actually issued though as only references to this have been found in the Lone Star catalogue for 1966. No actual sets have turned up whilst

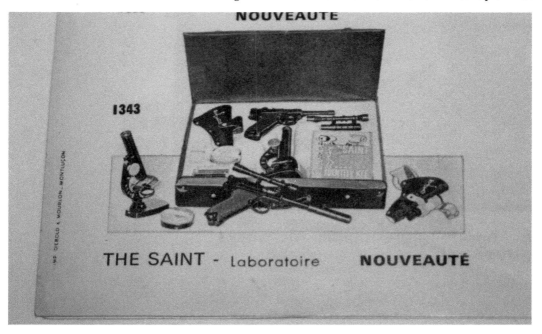

Saint lab set in French Lone Star catalogue.

carrying out research. According to the catalogue it 'contains the complete sleuth's back room equipment. A real microscope, an identity kit for building up the suspect's picture, fingerprint powder, marking pencils. The Saint's own pistol with telescopic sight and silencer, and holster with special spring clip. All packed into a strong useable PVC case.'

The Saint's Pistol Lone Star 1967

This is the same child's cap gun made of die-cast metal, shaped like a Luger 9 mm automatic. The only difference between this and the 1966 issue is the silencer; the long, thin style of silencer has now been replaced with a short dump style one.

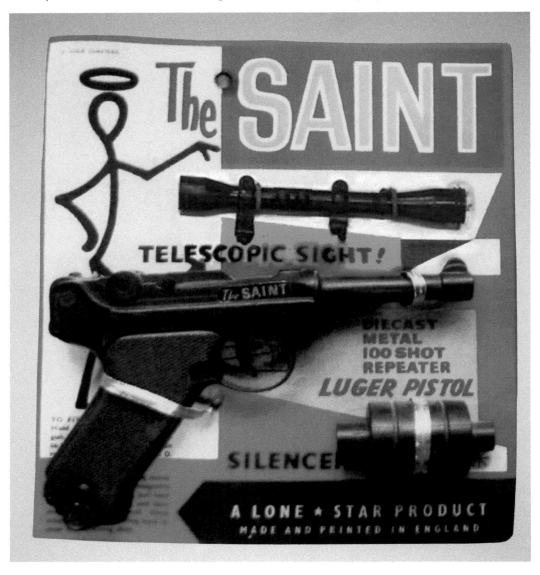

Second style Lone Star pistol. (Stuart James McKell)

Comparison of Lone Star silencers.

The Saint's Gun and Holster Set Lone Star 1967

Once again, this set, except for the change in style of silencer, is the same as the 1966 issue. Strangely, after this change in style of silencer, the 1969 Lone Star catalogue reverts to showing the first style from 1966.

Saint four-piece Rifle Lone Star 1968

Lone star introduced another saint pistol in 1968, this time it was based on a Walther P38 and came with a telescopic sight and the earlier style of thin silencer. It also had a shoulder stock, but of a completely different design to any that appears to have been used in any of Lone Star's other gun sets. It is also interesting to note that this item appears to have been issued on a different illustrated backing card to previous Lone Star Saint sets. This one featuring an image of Roger Moore, whilst previous backing car solely had text and the stick man logo.

Lone Star Saint four-piece rifle 1968 Lone Star catalogue.

The Saint Shooting Game Merit 1966

The firm of J&L Randall Ltd also known as Merit produced shooting game in 1967. This was basically a very nicely illustrated card backdrop with a sprung loaded action, which came with a plastic gun that fired suction tip darts. The intention was that you fired said darts at the centrally placed illustration of a stick of Dynamite, which when hit would cause the villains boat to 'explode' (well spring off the base). This not the only shooting game to be produced by Merit, they also created a near identical game for *The Avengers*, which, instead of a boat, featured a car. Both the target and the box lid featured the same illustration of Roger Moore throwing a stick of dynamite towards a speedboat in the background.

Shooting Game, Merit. (Stuart James McKell)

Confectionery/Trade Cards

Collecting trading cards has always been popular since they were first introduced with cigarettes back in late Victorian times. By the 1960s cards were a popular giveaway with all sorts of products, most commonly in the UK bubble gum. So, it seems inevitable that a series as popular as *The Saint* should end up as a set of cards. Around the world several different sets appear to have been produced, and *The Saint* also appeared as the odd card in larger sets covering several different series.

In the UK a set of seventy-two black and white photographic cards was issued by the bubble gum company Somportex in 1966. Two cards were issued in each pack with a stick of gum. Each card was sized 80 mm x 55 mm approximately. The backs of these cards included details of a Saint competition. It was also possible to send for a Saint signet ring by sending twelve wrappers along with a stamped addressed envelope to Somportex.

The same set of cards issued by Somportex was also issued in Denmark by Dandy Gum, though the cards in this issue were of a slightly smaller size than their UK equivalent.

In Spain a larger set of ninety-six cards was issued. Two versions of this Spanish set by Robert Jubal are known to exist. Firstly, a set printed on card with blank backs, then a second version printed on paper stock with a printed back. This Spanish issued set also had an album produced for keeping the cards in.

In Holland, Monty Gum issued at least sixteen full colour trading cards featuring the Saint, which were possibly part of a larger set containing images from other TV shows. Interestingly, according to sources these were issued with chocolate cookies rather than gum.

Somportex wrapper.

Somportex cards.

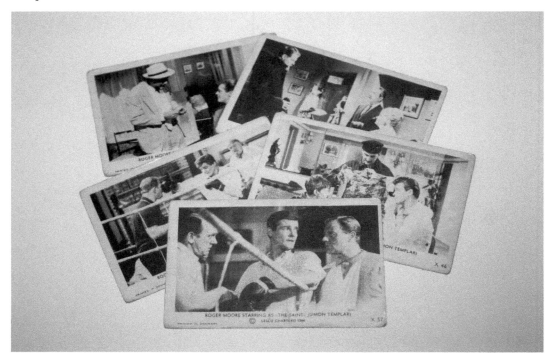

Dandy cards.

Right: Spanish card album.
(Remco Admiraal)

Below: Spanish cards.

Monty Gum cards.

Letraset.

Saint disc.

In 1971 Letraset produced at least ten small rubdown transfer sheets featuring the Saint. It appears that these are part of a much larger set issued in Sweden by the company Semic Press, who are now part of the Dutch publishing company Egmont. Sold in packs of several transfers much like trading cards, the set consisted in total of 252 images from a vast range of different cartoons and shows, ranging from Andy Capp to Yogi Bear. Each transfer is approx. 1 5/8-inch x 2 3/8-inch in size. Semic Press also produced an album for collectors to keep their transfers in.

A set of card discs featuring cartoon images from different TV shows was issued in Argentina during the 1960s and several cards in the set featured the Saint. The cards measure approximately 1 7/8-inch in diameter and have blank backs. It is possible that these were actually milk bottle caps, but this has not been confirmed.

The company Victoria issued cards featuring Roger Moore as the Saint in two different sets. These cards were issued with chocolate biscuits in Belgium. Also in Belgium, once again possibly part of a larger set featuring other series, cards were issued with Samo chips; what we in the UK would call crisps.

In Germany a set of cards called Show Top Stars, produced by Bergmann-Verlag, featured at least one image of Roger Moore.

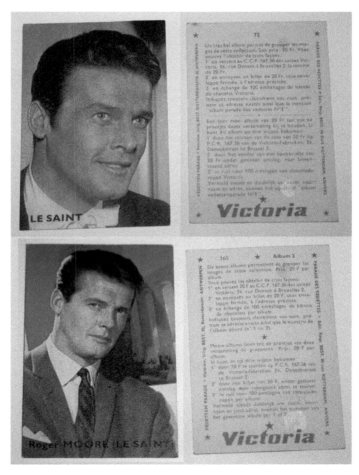

Victoria cards.

Samo chips card.

Show Top Stars card.

Records

The Edwin Astley-composed *Saint* theme has seen several issues over the years both as a single and on compilation LPs of various TV themes.

Singles

The Saint/Dr Finlay's Case book. Cover versions of the themes from both series recorded by the Les Reed strings on Piccadilly 7N.35080 in 1962.

Danger Man Theme/*The Saint* RCA Victor (RCA 1492) released in 1965 in the UK. This recording was by the theme's composer Edwin Astley. This single was previously issued in New Zealand in 1964, as High Wire (theme from *Danger Man*)/*The Saint* on RCA Victor 60409.

Piccadilly single.

RCA single.

The Saint/Lucifer recorded by the group the Shake Spears on the Belgium label Ronnex Records, R1366 in 1966. There appear to be several issues of this single; some have a red sleeve whilst others have a blue sleeve. Some copies have a credit for Sabam on the record label. This recording was issued in several different countries with different picture sleeves, including Italy where it was released on RT Club RT1522 (this edition was also possibly released in Turkey as Sayan RT1522). In the Netherlands it was issued on Fontanna 278120YF, whilst in Denmark Ronnex Records released it as STU42251. This single was re-released in the early 1970s being credited to Gene Latter and the Shake Spears.

Also released in the Netherlands was a cover version of *The Saint* theme by the Maskers, which appeared on the B side to their rendition of the *Batman* theme, Artone DS25.376.

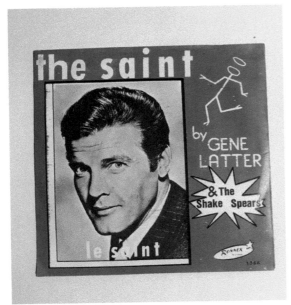

Above left: Shake Spears' red sleeve. (Remco Admiraal)

Above right: Dutch Fontana issue. (Remco Admiraal)

Left: Shake Spears' blue sleeve 1970s issue. (Remco Admiraal)

Right: 'Where Does Love Go' UK issue.

Below: 'Then the Saint Appeared' single.

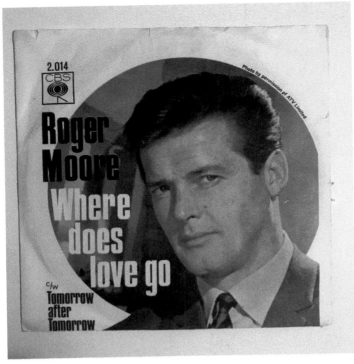

'Where Does Love Go' Dutch issue. (Remco Admiraal)

In the UK Danny Davis and his Orchestra released their cover version of *The Saint* on MGM records (MGM 1277) in 1965, with the B side being the little bandits of Juarez.

Norway saw release of a recording by the Key Brothers and The Quivers in 1965. This appeared on the Troll label (TR 159) with the Norwegian title of *Og Sa Kom Helgenen Frem*, which translates as *Then the 'Saint' Appeared*. This single featured a picture sleeve showing the group with Roger Moore. Interestingly this song was written by Leiber and Stoller, who were responsible for composing hits for Elvis Presley amongst others.

Roger Moore himself put out a single in 1965 on the CBS label called *Where Does Love Go*, which saw release not only in the UK but also in Norway and the Netherlands, the track apparently having come from the film of the same name. Roger's backing on this record was from Les Reed and his orchestra. The B side featured a track called 'Tomorrow after Tomorrow', for which Roger is credited as writer.

LPs and EPs

The EP *Top TV Themes* (NEP24276) released by Pye records in 1966 features a version of *The Saint* theme credited to the Eliminators, along with five other themes including *Z Cars* and *Thunderbirds*.

One other EP known to exist is *Temas de TV*, which was released in Mexico in 1969. As well as *The Saint* theme this also included themes for *The Champions, Department S* and *The Avengers*.

In the USA, Edwin Astley and his orchestra had an LP, *The Saint: Music from the TV series* released by RCA Victor in 1966. This album was available either in mono (LPM 3631) or stereo (LSP 3631). This featured the series theme along with other pieces of music that had been composed for the show.

Top TV Themes EP.
(Remco Admiraal)

*Themes for Secret
Agents* LP.

Phase 4 World of Thrillers LP.

RCA Victor also issued an album *Secret Agent Meets The Saint*. This 1965 album featured Edwin Astley tracks used on the Saint album as well as tracks from another British TV series *Danger Man* (known in the USA as *Secret Agent*). Once again available in either mono (LPM 3467) or stereo (LSP 3467).

Themes for Secret Agents by The Roland Shaw Orchestra, 'Phase 4 Stereo' PFS 4094 released in 1968. Cover version *The Saint* theme along with versions of several James Bond themes, *I Spy*, *The Man from U.N.C.L.E.*, *The Avengers* and others.

The Phase 4 World of Thrillers by Roland Shaw and his Orchestra, Decca SPA 160. Released in 1971 this featured the same cover version of *The Saint* theme as used on Shaw's previous album.

Top TV Themes. This album, released on the Marble Arch label (MAL 1179) in 1969, features a cover version of *The Saint* theme by Cyril Stapleton and The Eliminators, along with versions of themes from *The Champions* and *Department S*, by other artists.

Time for TV by Brian Fahey and his Orchestra, Columbia Studio 2 Stereo TWO 175. Released in 1967, this album contains a cover version of *The Saint* theme along with renditions of *The Avengers, The Baron, The Man From U.N.C.L.E., Danger Man* and *Thunderbirds*. This LP has a very nice picture sleeve showing *The Avengers*.

Top TV Themes LP.

Magazines/Comics

Around the world so many different magazines and comics have featured the Saint in one way or another that it would be impossible to cover all of them in detail within the space allowed in this book, so these are just a few.

Starting with British comics to have featured the Saint, Thorpe and Porter put out a series of four black and white comics in the early 1960s. The artist Mick Anglo has been credited with much of the art in these comics, which were reprinted in several different countries by different publishers.

Diana, a comic aimed primarily at girls and published by DC Thomson & Co. Ltd in 1966, issued a free gift in an issue of the comic. *Diana's Top Secret Diary* was a small, soft cover booklet with photos of *The Avengers, The Man from U.N.C.L.E., Danger Man, The Saint,* James Bond (plus others) and included various simple codes.

The Saint featured as a regular strip story in *TV Tornado* magazine, published by City Magazines. Starting in issue 15, 22 April 1967, most issues would contain a two-page black and white strip based on the series. This first story was entitled 'The Informer' and the Saint's arrival was heralded on the comic's editorial page as well as the Saint being featured on the front cover montage. The Saint would regularly appear on these cover montages, being given his first full cover with issue 20, and would appear on the comics cover a total of seventeen times. While the Saint strip story did miss a few issues the Saint

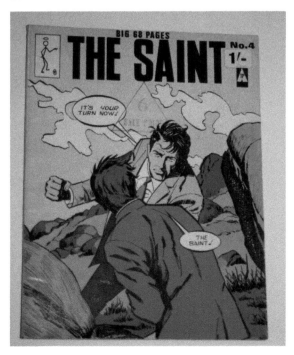

British comic No. 4.

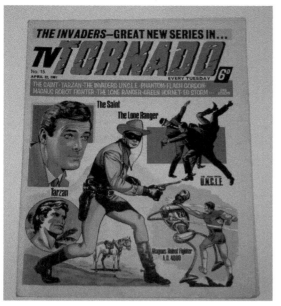

Above left: First *TV Tornado* to feature the Saint.

Above right: First full Saint cover on *TV Tornado*.

Right: TV Tornado covers.

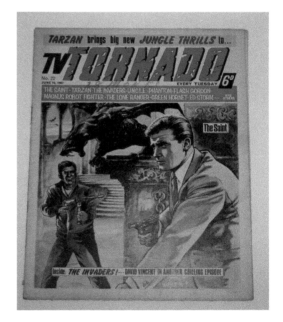

would remain in *TV Tornado*, the strip notably being replaced in issues 50 and 55 with photographic features on the series, until its demise with issue 88. This being said, the comic's last issue, upon which point it merged into *TV Century 21* comic starting with issue 192. The Saint, however, had moved across a couple of weeks earlier, starting his run in the comic with a story entitled 'The Treasure Hunters' in issue 190. The character would remain a regular in this title, with his last appearance being in issue 230 in June 1969.

The Saint would then reappear a few months later in the newly launched *TV21 & Joe 90* comic, starting in issue 1 during September of 1969 with the strip story 'Meet the Saint'.

59

Above left and right: TV Tornado covers.

Left: Last *TV Tornado* to feature the Saint on the cover.

He would survive in this comic for around a further fifty issues before eventually disappearing from its pages.

Look-in Independent Television Publications. Several issues of this children's comic/TV listings magazine featured pieces on the series, or rather on Roger Moore who also appeared on the front cover for the issue dated 14 August 1971. The magazine also featured him in the Christmas edition that year dated 25 December, as he did in the following week's cover dated 1 January 1972 and in the 9 September edition. Original price per issue was 5p.

Right: *TV Century 21* 190.

Below: *TV21 & Joe 90* comics.

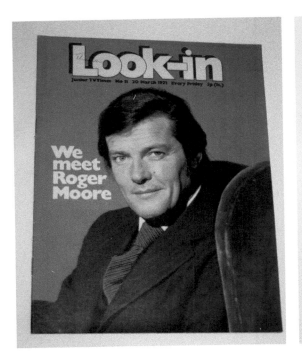

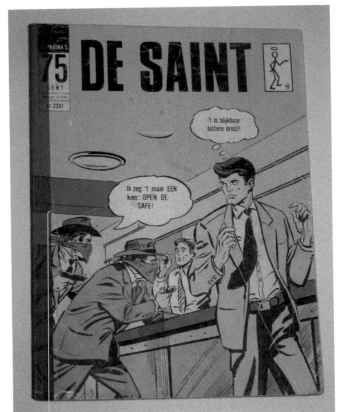

Above left: *Look-in* comic
20 March 1971.

Above right: French comic.
(Remco Admiraal)

Left: Dutch comic.

Spanish comic.

In the UK The Saint had predominantly been a strip within various comics. Over in Europe the Saint would star in his own titled comics in several countries. *Le Saint* would appear in at least thirteen issues of his own comic in France between 1970 and 1972, published under the *Les editions de Poche* banner. Covers featured an illustrated Roger Moore Saint. In the Netherlands Classics Nederland N. V. published four issues of *De Saint*, reprinting material from the UK Thorpe and Porter comics.

Likewise, the Thorpe and Porter strips were reprinted in Denmark by TP Forlget between 1967 and 1968, *Helgenen* was his moniker there, where at least fifteen issues were produced. In Norway over 250 issues of *Helgenen* were produced from 1966, running all the way through to 1989. The title changed publishers three times along the way. El Santo appeared in at least thirteen issues of his own title published by Editorial Ferma in Spain, while in Finland, where *The Saint* was known as *Pyhimys*, he appeared in around seven issues of his own title. At least four issues, Thorpe and Porter reprints, of a *Simon Templer* comic appeared in German. Finally, in Sweden the Saint also had a very long running comic, where *Helgonet* ran between 1966 and 1985 clocking up 227 issues for the publishing company Semic Press.

The Saint was also a regular strip in the Dutch equivalent of *TV Century 21* comic, *TV2000*. This comic was mainly reprints of its British counterpart, though it did feature original cover artwork, upon which Roger Moore's Saint would often appear.

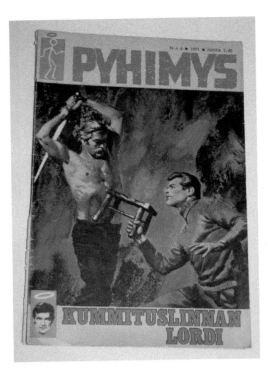

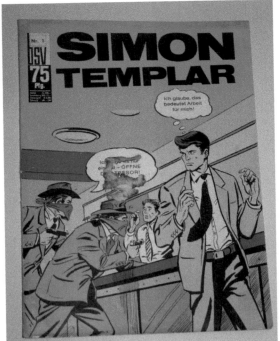

Above left: Finnish comic.

Above right: German comic.

Left: German comic.

Above left and right: German comic.

Right: Swedish comic. (Remco Admiraal)

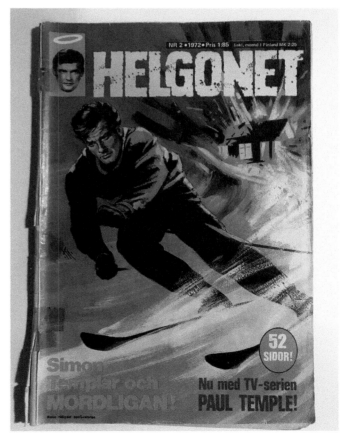

Left: Swedish comic.
(Remco Admiraal)

Below: Dutch *TV 2000.*
(Remco Admiraal)

Above left: *TVTimes Extra.*

Above Right: *Poster Magazine.*

Right: Dutch TV guide
25 January 1964.
(Remco Admiraal)

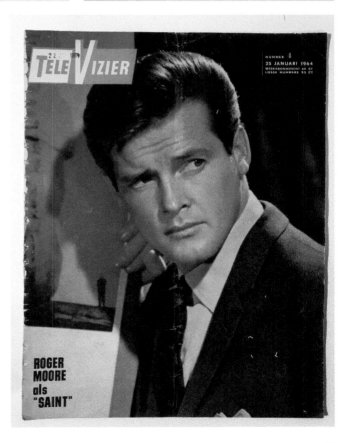

Above left: Dutch TV guide 28 February 1965. (Remco Admiraal)

Above right: *Bravo* magazine 2 November 1970. (Remco Admiraal)

Left: Spanish variety magazine 25 November 1967. (Remco Admiraal)

Moving on to a few of the many magazines featuring pieces on the Saint, *Weekend & Today* (Associated Newspapers Ltd.) No. 3120, dated 9 Dec 1964, would feature an article, 'The Saint Isn't Naughty Enough for Me' reputedly by Roger Moore.

TV Times (Independent Television Publications) produced a special magazine in 1972. Priced at 15p, *The Roger Moore story* covered Roger's career up to this point, including a very healthy section on his time on *The Saint*, along with a large piece on his new series *The Persuaders*.

The following year in 1973 Poster Magazines Publishers Ltd produced a one issue *Roger Moore Poster Magazine* devoted to his career, mostly concentrating on *The Saint* and *The Persuaders*, but it also covered Roger's newest role of James Bond in *Live and Let Die*. Originally priced at 25p.

The Saint appeared on magazine covers all around the world, including Dutch TV guides, the German teen magazine *Bravo* and various Spanish variety magazine, several of which carried articles on Roger, who received the Premio Radiofonico best actor award for 1966–1967 in Barcelona.

As was the case with most TV shows at the time the theme was released in sheet music form, both in its own right and in a book containing several other themes by Robbins Music Corp. Ltd in 1965.

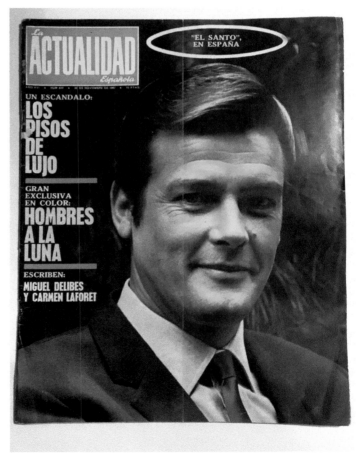

Spanish variety magazine
30 November 1967.
(Remco Admiraal)

Miscellaneous

Postcards were produced in several countries in France by Pok – Publistar Bruxelles, while in Spain they appear to have been produced by Hospitalet (Barcelona).

A promotional brandy hanging postcard also appeared in Spain during 1968. Roger Moore had appeared in a series of newspaper and magazine adverts for brandy. During this promotion a postcard was attached to the brandy bottles.

Above: Spanish postcards.

Left: Spanish brandy promotion.

Matchbox labels. (Remco Admiraal)

Glass tumbler.

Left: Plastic badge.

Below: Bottle cap.

Matchbox labels featuring the Saint appeared in the Netherlands. Originating in Spain, but aimed at the English-speaking market, a glass tumbler featuring Roger Moore's image and the stick man logo appeared as did a small plastic badge.

In Australia the firm Coca-Cola issued a series of different bottle caps in the late 1960s/ early 1970s featuring stars of various TV shows printed on the inside of the cap. At least two bottle caps featured images of Roger Moore, one as the Saint the other from his earlier series *Ivanhoe*.

As was the case with many ITC TV shows at the time, several episodes of the series were subsequently recut and released around the world for feature films. In the case of the Roger Moore *The Saint* series, two movies appeared; these were *Vendetta for the Saint* and *The Fiction Makers*. It is, however, interesting to note that in several European countries, due to the popularity of *The Saint* TV series, some non-Saint movies of Roger's were released with publicity material promoting them as if they were Saint movies. The Belgium poster for *Crossplot* being a prime example of this.

Right: Italian poster
Vendetta for the Saint.

Below: Italian poster
The Fiction Makers.

Left: Italian poster *The Fiction Makers*.

Below left: Australian poster *Vendetta for the Saint*.

Below right: Belgium poster *Crossplot*.

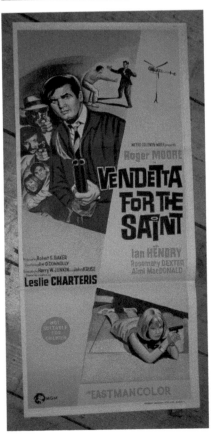

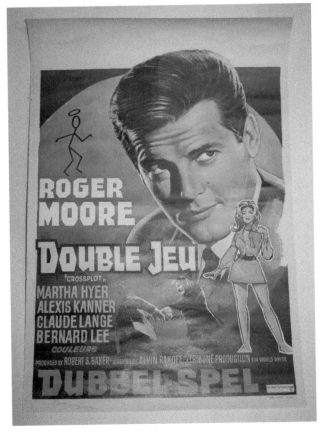

Return of the Saint ITC 1978–1979

Leslie Charteris' hero, the Saint, was to return to television screens in the mid-1970s, but no longer was Roger Moore at the helm as the debonair hero, the role instead now taken by Ian Ogilvy. Twenty-four episodes of *Return of the Saint* were produced, the show being broadcast on ITV over the winter period of 1978–1979. It had been coproduced by ITC and the Italian broadcaster RAI and unlike its predecessor, which had been almost entirely filmed in the UK despite being set around the world, this series featured extensive location shooting around Europe.

Ian Ogilvy was interviewed in 2017 about the series and how getting the part had come about:

> My agent called me to say that Bob Baker thought I'd be good to take over from Roger Moore in *The Saint*. It had been off the air for several years. I thought, 'Oh, right, really.' It turned out his wife had seen me in *Upstairs, Downstairs* and it was odd really because the two characters of the Saint and the character I play in *Upstairs, Downstairs* could not have been more different. But the reason was, of course, that I looked a bit like Roger, there's no denying it, and so it was on that basis, then I didn't hear anything at all, because Bob Baker said he hadn't yet got the green light for it at all, he'd got to persuade his boss, Lew

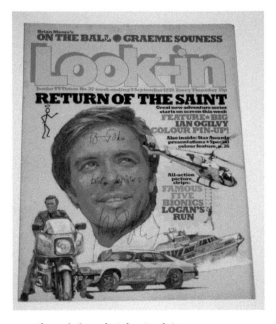 

Above left and right: Look-in.

Grade, and it took him another six or seven years. Then all of a sudden my agent said you've been offered *The Saint*. I went, 'Great!' and that's how easy it was. I never did an audition, I never read for it, I just had a meeting with him one year, then all those years later the offer was there. Which is the best kind of work, isn't it?

I never met Lew Grade. The man was paying my bills and I never met him. I only met his wife once and that was because she asked me to do a charity 'MC' job. I think he hated the show and I don't think he liked me in it... He was the one that said no to the second series and yet it was crazy, because we were in profit and we'd sold it to god knows how many countries. The accountants were delirious, but he just said no, I don't want to do it anymore. It was very expensive. It was ridiculous really, all the crew and I, we never said goodbye, because we expected to see each other in about three or four months.

I think the main thing different between mine and Roger's show was that Roger's stayed firmly at Elstree studios and went on the backlot occasionally, but by the time we did *The Saint* Bob Baker realised that we had to spend money actually on real locations. When the car was driving along it had to be a real car driving along a real road. I mean Roger had a bush which was revolving! So styles of television had changed. As to whether or not fashion had, I wouldn't know that. I was again relentlessly trendy at the beginning, we went to this shop in Jermyn Street. Oh I hated most of these clothes! The one good thing I think Lew Grade did do was to say, 'No, come on, suits, plain classic suits.' That was good. But other than that, I think the style of what was expected by a television audience had changed, so they expected more glamorous locations, real locations, not just a studio backlot and sets, which is what Roger did.

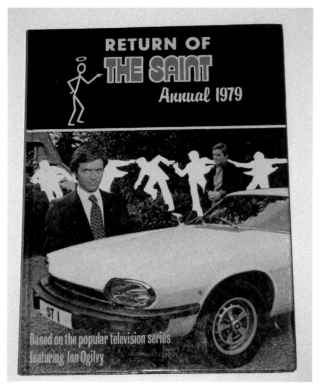

1979 annual.

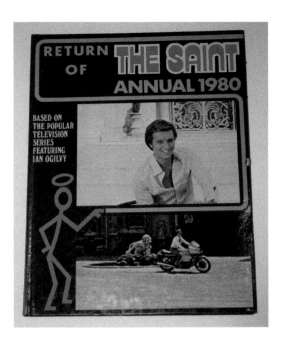

1980 annual.

The nice thing was, there was a gap of several years between it, but I knew there'd be comparisons between us and I recognised it as being what we called a personality job, you know, it's like Bond, it's whatever you make it. I just thought the Saint was a straightforward hero character I was playing, I must try and inject some humour into it a bit if I can. But what Roger had done worked really well and while I didn't imitate Roger I thought it worked for him, and also the scripts were all written by the same people. A lot of them were rehashed, he did sort of not quite Nazi spies, we did the same scripts but with the Red September gang. I learnt Scuba diving on *The Saint* actually.

I was taught that, but horse riding I'd done since I was a little boy. We did a skiing episode and they said to me, 'You are absolutely not allowed to move on the insistence of the insurance company, you just have to stand there.' But after a while I got bored and said to the assistant director, 'How long are you going to be on the set up for the next shot?' He said an hour, so I said how about if I just went off quietly, if I promise to be back in half an hour, and he said, 'I didn't hear you say that Ian, bye'. And I started skiing again, but very very quietly as I shouldn't have been doing it. Little things like that. And riding horses that's true. You know it's always amused me about the Saint that he could drive any car, he could ride a motorcycle ... I put the motorcycle in by the way. I said to Bob, 'You've got to have a motorbike in this.' I suggested it to him and he went, 'Yeah alright.' But he didn't really approve.

The Saint had been introduced to a new generation and a host of new products were released to cash in on this new series, interestingly many of the items were not branded as *Return of the Saint* but just simply as *The Saint*.

The adventures in this series were different from the Roger Moore series in that they were original teleplays not based on any of the Charteris stories, though several would be adapted as books, giving Charteris the writing credit.

Books

British Annuals

As with the original series children's annuals were produced, though this time not by World Distributors, but instead by Stafford Pemberton Publishing, who produced two annuals.

The first *Return of The Saint Annual*, published in 1979 with an original cover price of £1.50, had a green spine and a photographic cover which featured images of Ian Ogilvy and the Jaguar XJS. While the second *Return of* 'The Saint Annual', published in 1980 at an original cover price of £1.75, has a red spine with a photographic cover showing two images; one of Ian Ogilvy as the Saint and the other showing him seated upon a motorcycle. This second annual appears to be slightly harder to obtain that its predecessor.

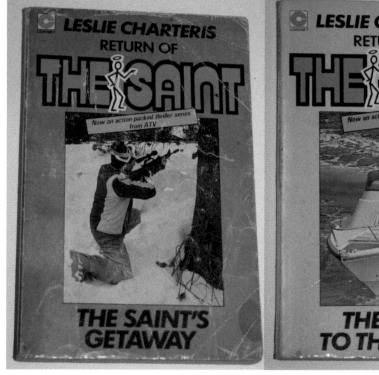

UK paperbacks.

British Paperbacks

At least eight Saint paperbacks were issued in the UK to tie in with the new Ian Ogilvy series. These were issued by Coronet Books in 1978 at a price of 75p each. All of them have a colour photograph from the series on their respective covers. While all are edited by L. Charteris, some are reissues of original Charteris novels, others are adaptations of various TV episodes from both the 1960s series and the then current 'Return of' series. Titles released at the time included *The Saint and the Hapsurg Necklace* by C. Short, *The Saint and the Templer Treasure* by Donne Avenell and Graham Weaver, *Trust The Saint* by L. Charteris, *Send for The Saint* by P. Bloxfom (this title was two episodes of the *Return of The Saint* TV series novelised, being based on the episodes 'The Midas Double and The Porn Gambit'), *The Saint in Trouble* by G. Weaver (two more *Return of the Saint* TV episodes novelised, 'The Imprudent Professor' and 'The Red Sabbath', and *The Saint Abroad* by Fleming Lee, this time two episodes from the 1960s TV series, 'The Art Collectors' and 'The Persistent Patriots'. The last two Saint books also known to have been issued with *Return of the Saint* covers were *The Saint to the Rescue* by L. Charteris and *The Saint's Getaway* by L. Charteris, which were both reissues of previously existing titles.

Severn House Publishers Ltd issued eight hardbacks with Ian Ogilvy *Return of the Saint* covers in 1980: *Thanks to the Saint, The Saint Sees it Through, The Saint Bids Diamonds, The Saint Steps In, The Saint Plays With Fire, The Saint In London, Senor Saint* and *The Saint on Guard*. Then a further two titles were issued in 1986, again with Ogilvy covers. These were *Call for the Saint* and *Alias the Saint*.

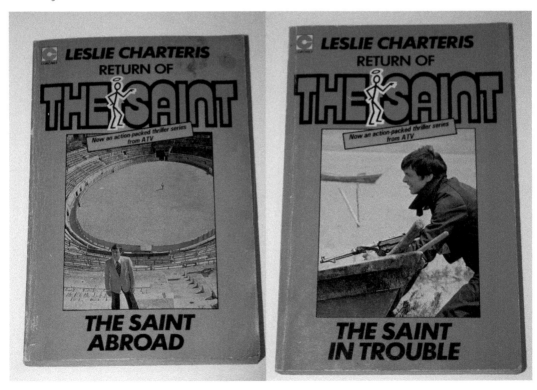

UK paperbacks.

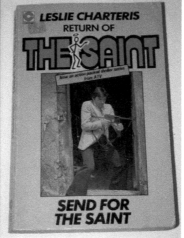

UK paperbacks.

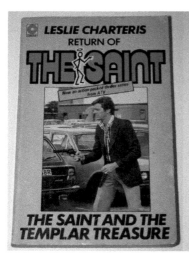
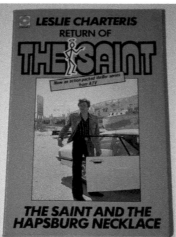

Left: UK paperbacks.

Below: UK hardbacks.
(Jaz Wiseman)

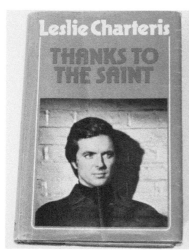
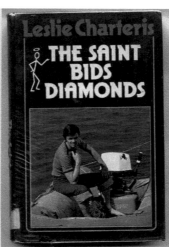

Dutch Paperbacks

In the Netherland three of *The Saint* novels were issued with covers to tie in with the *Return of the Saint* series, they were published by *Zwarte Beertjes*. The titles published were *De Saint in de Knel, De Saint en de schat van de tempeliers* and *Op de Saint Kun je rekenen*.

Above left , above right and right: Dutch paperback.

Toys and Games

Saint Jaguar large.

Interestingly, while produced to tie in with the new *Return of the Saint* TV series, several of the products produced at the time were issued simply under *The Saint* banner, rather than as *Return of the Saint*. The most popular thing from the series to produce a toy of was the Saint's car, and this time around it was a Jaguar XJS.

Corgi seems to have had almost the sole concession on Saint Jaguars in 1978, producing three different sized versions of it that year.

Corgi Models

The Saint's Jaguar XJS, Corgi Toys 1978. Corgi's first issue of the Jaguar, issued in October of 1978, was in their standard approximately 1/43-inch scale sized range. This die-cast model of the car used by the Saint in the series was produced in white with *The Saint* logo on the bonnet, its only feature being opening doors. This was issued at an original price of £1.65. There do appear to be two different versions of the packaging for this model: most examples of this have a box quite brightly printed with a yellow interior to the box, whilst other examples have a much more darkly printed box containing a dark blue almost black interior.

The second version of Saint's Jaguar XJS produced that year by Corgi Toys was a Corgi Jr (No. 32 in the range). This had die-cast bodywork, painted white with *The Saint* logo on bonnet in black with a red plastic interior and black plastic base plate. The model came bubble packed with the backing card showing the real car in action. Very little to tie the model in with series if found loose other than logo on bonnet.

The model also saw release on a different bubble card which was little more than a base for the car to stand on with a plastic bubble enclosing it. This smaller version was priced at 60p.

Saint Jaguar. (Vectis)

Corgi Jr.

Corgi Jr variant
packaging.

Above: Sonic Jaguar.

Left: Corgi Jr set. (Vectis)

Below: Sonic Jaguar guns.

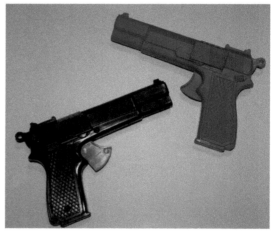

This small Corgi Juniors edition did also appear packaged with four other models as part of a heroes gift pack of models.

The final version of the Saint's Jaguar XJS by Corgi Toys, also issued in 1978, was a Sonic Control model. This is a large plastic battery operated model, which changes direction of travel in response to the clicking of a small plastic gun also included in the box. The car is white with once again *The Saint* logo on the bonnet, and number plates ST 1. This is a great model of the Jaguar, but the means of control is a little dodgy to say the least. There are two known variations of this toy, one contains a black plastic clicker gun, while the other set contains a red plastic gun. One last thing to mention is that the model shown on the box photograph is presumably the prototype model, as it appears to show several differences to the finished model that was issued.

Revell Model Kit

Revell did attempt to break Corgi's monopoly on Jaguars, producing a plastic model kit in 1978 of the Saint's Jaguar XJS. This was produced in white, black and chromed plastic parts so that the kit could be built up with no painting required.

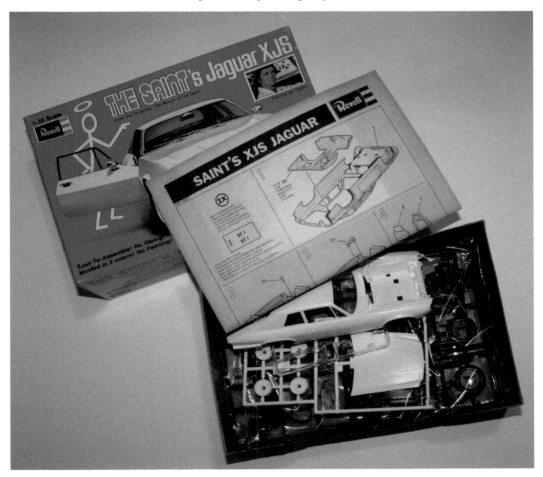

Revell kit.

Above left: Pendant.

Above right: Badge.

Crescent Toys

The largest range of *Return of the Saint* products issued were by the firm Crescent Toys, who produced several different items for the series.

The Saint, Pendant, Crescent Toys, 1978

A fairly large die-cast metal medallion was issued by Crescent, which appears to have been sold in a small plastic bag with a card slipped inside behind this quite hefty item.

Pistol.

The Saint, **Badge, Crescent Toys, 1978**

This die-cast metal badge of *The Saint* logo seems to have been made from the same mould as the medallion, as it is near identical in size. This was issued on a large blue printed backing card.

Return of the Saint, **Pistol, Crescent Toys, 1978**

This die-cast 100 shot, snub nose revolver cap gun came issued in a small card box displaying images of Ian Ogilvy and the Jaguar XJS. There are no markings on this toy gun

Gun and holster set.

anywhere to show that it is related to any TV series, and Crescent did release this small gun for other series as well.

Return of the Saint, Gun and Holster Set, Crescent Toys, 1978

Crescent would issue this same 100 shot cap gun on a photographic backing card with a faux leather belt and holster. The backing card showed the Saint dangling underneath a helicopter with an insert photograph of Ian Ogilvy in the role.

Crescent issued one other boxed set. This originally came shrunk wrapped in an open fronted box. The box head photograph shows the Saint in action in a launch with, once again, the small insert photograph. This set contained a snub-nosed cap gun, different from Crescent's other sets, whereas the other Saint guns issued by them were 100 shot cap guns using the old paper roles of caps. The gun in this set contained eight shot ring caps. Once again, the faux leather holster, complete with stick man logo, was included but additional to this set were a pair of die-cast metal hand-cuffs, the Saint badge that Crescent had previously issued on its own and a small plastic wallet/ID card.

Boxed set.

Gun comparison.

The Saint Mission Kit, Thomas Salter, 1978

This is an incredibly rare set. Half of the box lid is window fronted through which most of the set's contents can be viewed, while down the other half of the lid is an almost full-length photograph of Ian Ogilvy as the Saint. This kit is so typically mid-1970s in its style with working plastic binoculars. It also contained a plastic gun, silencer, holster, hand grenade (squirts water) and assorted cardboard cut-outs that made up two code breakers along with several other items.

Appearing in a trade catalogue for 1979, but seemingly never produced, was a *Return of the Saint* board game. Little is known about this item – possibly produced by Palitoy. While a Greek board game was definitely produced, this Greek *Επιστροφή του Αγίου* game was little more than a cheap rehash of Cludo.

Thomas Salter Mission Kit.

Magazines/Comics

Unlike the original series, the *Return of the Saint* did not appear as a comic strip in any UK comics. Features on the series did however appear in several magazines. *TV Detectives* poster magazine devoted the entirety of its eighth issue to the series. Cover price for this magazine was 40p.

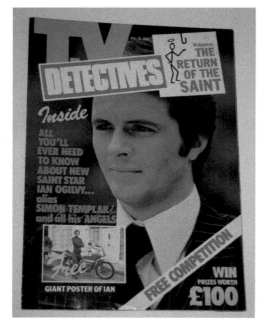

Above left: *TV Detectives* poster magazine.

Above right: *Weekend Extra.*

Left: TVTimes

Weekend Extra, published by Associated Newspapers Group Ltd, was one of several magazines to feature an article on the new Saint, which they did in their spring 1978 edition, when Ian Ogilvy appeared on the cover. The short article was accompanied by a Charteris story *The Saint and the Prince of Cherkessia*.

TV Times Independent Television Publications Ltd

The ITV television listings magazine *TVTimes* (cover dated 7 September 1978) featured the series upon its launch, with both a cover feature and a short Saint story by Charteris, entitled *The Russian Prisoner*. *TVTimes* magazine also published an edition of *TVTimes Extra* in 1979 called *Who's Who Among the TV Super Sleuths*. This included features on *Starsky & Hutch*, *The Six Million Dollar Man*, *Hazell*, *The Sweeny*, *Kojak*, *The New Avengers*, *Target*, *The Professionals*, *Charlies Angels*, *CHIPS*, *Hawaii Five-0*, *Vegas*, *The Incredible Hulk* plus many others. Most notably it also included a text *Return of the Saint* story, *The Saint and the Senorita's Quest*. All for the princely price of 35p.

British Comics

Look-in Comic Independent Television Publications Ltd. The *Return of the Saint* appeared on the cover of four issues of *Look-in* comic, normally with the issue containing a full colour pin-up of Ian Ogilvy as well. The first was around the series debut in the 9 September 1978 dated issue, while the show's other appearances in the magazine were on 28 October 1978, 6 January 1979 and 12 July 1980.

Four of IPC Magazines Ltd's comics teamed up on issues cover dated 2 December 1978 to run a joint competition to win a Corgi Toys model of Saint's Jaguar. Each of the four comics involved in this cross promotion featured an almost full cover of their respective title devoted to the competition with full details inside the comic. The four titles involved with the promotion were: *Cheeky*, *Buster*, *Whoopee* and *Whizzer & Chips*.

 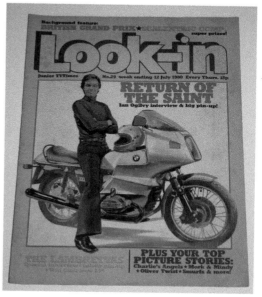

Above left and right: Look-in cover.

IPC magazine's great rivals DC Thomson & Co. would, a week later on 9 December, also feature *Return of the Saint* in one of their girls' comics, *Emma*. Devoting the cover that week to a competition to win a girl's two-tone zipped Saint top. Thirty of these tops could be won in a range of four different colour combinations and three sizes. This same issue also included an interview with Ian Ogilvy. *Emma* must have had a few of the tops left over as a couple of months later on 17 February 1979 the comic would run another competition to win the same two-tone Saint zipped top. The *Return of the Saint* featured once more in *Emma* comic in July of that year with another small piece on Ian Ogilvy.

Four comic competitions.

Right: *Emma* cover.

Below: *Emma* competition.

Records

Singles

Rather than reuse the original *The Saint* theme by Edwin Astley, a new theme was composed for the *Return of the Saint* by John Scott. This was released on Pye Records (7N 46127) in 1978 with a picture sleeve. The artists credited were The Saint Orchestra. Most copies of this single have a pink/purple colour gradient label on the record, but some copies do have a grey label. These grey labelled copies appear to have come in a plain Pye record sleeve rather than the colour picture sleeve.

UK single.

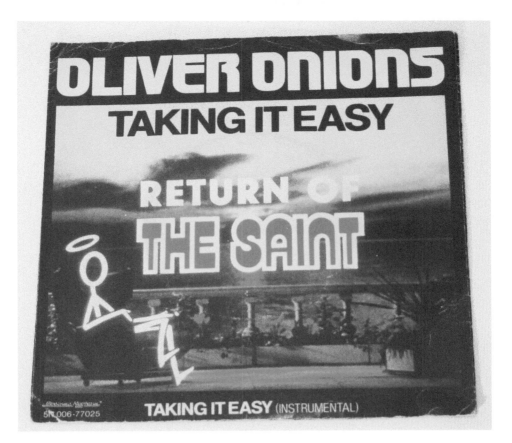

German single.

In Europe a completely different theme was used for the series. This was a song called 'Takin' it Easy', performed by the group Olivers Onions. The song was released as a single with a picture sleeve in several countries around the world. It was released on the EMI label in Germany (EMI 1C 006-77 025), France (EMI 2C 006-77 025) and Argentina as 'El Retorno Del Santo' (EMI 1684). While in the Netherland it was on the Bovema Negram label (5N 006 77025). All of these releases were in 1978. In Spain it was released a year later in 1979 on Reflejo (Reflejo 10 C 006-77025), as 'Tomalo Con Calma – Return Of The Saint – El Retorno Del Santo'.

This has been just a small dip into the wealth of items that have been produced over the years relating to one of fiction's most enduring heroes. As stated at the outset, this book has primarily devoted itself to the television incarnations of *The Saint* and space has prevented inclusion of so many items related not only to these TV incarnations but to the Saint in general. Over the years so many – both licensed and unlicensed – variations of the famous stick man logo have appeared in vast quantities of products, from cufflinks to garage-produced models of the Saint's Volvo. Then there are items relating to both the Simon Dutton series from 1989, as well as the Val Kilmer movie of the Saint. The Saint is an immortal character, and future film or TV adaptions will no doubt spawn many more products in the future. Even as this book was going to press it was announced that Dexter Fletcher was to remake *The Saint* for Paramount pictures.

Simon Dutton *TV Guide.*

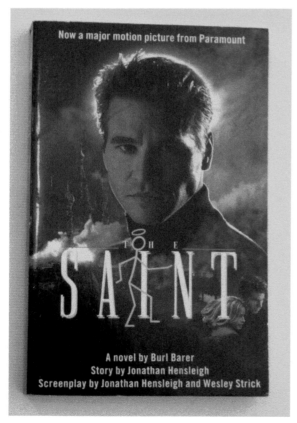

Val Kilmer *The Saint* paperback.